Clean Air to Share

Reader Consultants

Cheryl Norman Lane, M.A.Ed.
Classroom Teacher
Chino Valley Unified School District

Jennifer M. Lopez, M.S.Ed., NBCT
Teacher Specialist—History/Social Studies
Norfolk Public Schools

iCivics Consultants

Emma Humphries, Ph.D.
Chief Education Officer

Taylor Davis, M.T.
Director of Curriculum and Content

Natacha Scott, MAT
Director of Educator Engagement

Publishing Credits

Rachelle Cracchiolo, M.S.Ed., *Publisher*
Emily R. Smith, M.A.Ed., *VP of Content Development*
Véronique Bos, *Creative Director*
Dona Herweck Rice, *Senior Content Manager*
Dani Neiley, *Associate Content Specialist*
Fabiola Sepulveda, *Series Designer*

Image Credits: pp.6–9 Brian Martin; pp. 12-13 Bijit K. Dutta/Shutterstock ; p.17 Elisabeth Aardema/Shutterstock.com; p.21 Sundry Photography/ Shutterstock ; p.22 Rachael Warriner/Shutterstock; p.23 Brent Olson/Shutterstock; p.25 Antoine Ramus/Shutterstock; p.26 U.S. National Archives; p.28 Steve and Julie via Flickr; p.29 ZumaPress/Newscom; all other images from iStock and/or Shutterstock

Library of Congress Cataloging-in-Publication Data

Names: Jacobs, Parvaneh, author.
Title: Clean air to share / Parvaneh Jacobs, M.A.Sc.
Description: Huntington Beach, CA : Teacher Created Materials, [2021] | Includes index. | Audience: Grades 2-3. | Description based on print version record and CIP data provided by publisher; resource not viewed.
Identifiers: LCCN 2020016297 (print) | LCCN 2020016298 (ebook) | ISBN 9781087619385 (ebook) | ISBN 9781087605142 (paperback) |
Subjects: LCSH: Air--Pollution--Juvenile literature.
Classification: LCC TD883.13 (ebook) | LCC TD883.13 J33 2021 (print) | DDC 363.739/26--dc23
LC record available at https://lccn.loc.gov/2020016297

TCM | Teacher Created Materials

5482 Argosy Avenue
Huntington Beach, CA 92649-1039
www.tcmpub.com
ISBN 978-1-0876-0514-2

Table of Contents

Clean Air

Clean air is important for everyone. Without clean air, it is hard to breathe, go outside, or play outdoors. Not only do people need clean air, but plants and animals need it too.

When air is clean, the sky is clear. When air is clean, clean water falls when it rains. When air is clean, people are healthier, and they feel better.

clean air

Unclean air looks different from clean air. It might be filled with **pollution**. It might make everything look hazy. Unclean air makes it hard to see far away. Breathing can be hard as well when the air is unclean.

So, how do we keep our air clean? People are hard at work finding ways everyone can help.

polluted air

Jump into Fiction

Raheem Plants Trees

"Happy Arbor Day!" Mr. Murphy calls out as Raheem and his classmates find their seats. Raheem had only been in Mr. Murphy's class for a few weeks. He liked that the wacky teacher was always excited to start the day. Raheem didn't have a lot of friends yet, but Mr. Murphy made school fun anyway. Today, Mr. Murphy had drawn a ton of trees on the whiteboard. He was even dressed like a tree!

"Today, we are going to plant trees around the school," Mr. Murphy began. "Trees are the world's lungs. They help turn dirty air into clean, healthy air."

The more excited Mr. Murphy became, the more excited the class became too. Raheem remembered his old house, surrounded by trees. It was very easy to breathe there. He wanted everyone to feel that way.

Raheem and his class got to work. Mr. Murphy showed each student where to dig a hole for the tree they would plant. It was hard work! Ms. Barnes, the P.E. teacher, came over to help. After they finished digging, Ms. Barnes helped Raheem place a young tree into the hole he dug.

Mr. Murphy gave a watering can to Raheem.

"It will be up to each of you to make sure your tree grows and stays healthy," began Mr. Murphy. "Each leaf on a tree has the power to turn dirty air into clean air. As each tree matures, it will grow more leaves. That means it will get better at cleaning air!"

Raheem carefully poured water onto his newly planted tree. Today had been a lot of hard work, but he was glad they had done something good. When he got home, he planned on asking his parents if they could plant a tree too.

Back to Nonfiction

The Greenhouse Effect

A layer of air called the atmosphere surrounds Earth. When gases and dust get trapped there, the air becomes dirty. A lot of things **pollute** the atmosphere. One common form of pollution comes from cars.

When vehicles are running, they let off gases. One of those gases is **carbon dioxide**. It floats into the sky and gets trapped near a part of the atmosphere called the ozone layer. The ozone layer is like a shield for Earth. The ozone layer protects Earth's surface from the harmful effects of the sun.

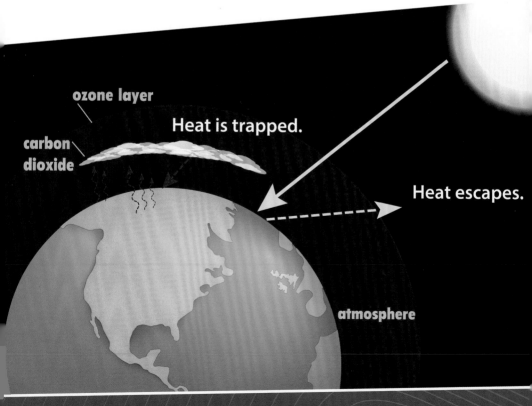

ozone layer

Heat is trapped.

carbon dioxide

Heat escapes.

atmosphere

When some gases, such as carbon dioxide, get trapped by the ozone layer, these gases can cause the ozone layer to thin. That means more of the sun's rays and heat reach Earth's surface. The temperature of the planet increases. The result is called the greenhouse effect.

Greenhouses help plants grow in cold climates. They trap heat inside. Earth's atmosphere acts like a greenhouse. It warms our planet by trapping heat. But too much heat is harmful to our planet. People are working to solve the problem of the greenhouse effect.

This greenhouse keeps the air inside warm.

Finding Solutions

Plants and trees use carbon dioxide as food. Trees can store the gas for decades! Trees and plants help lower the amount of gas in the atmosphere.

One man in India knew that trees could help Earth. He wanted to plant an entire forest. It took him decades of hard work. But Jadav "Molai" Payeng (JAW-dev moo-LIE PAW-yeng) finally met his goal! He has planted tens of thousands of trees. They now form the Molai Forest. Now, elephants, tigers, and rhinos live in the forest all year.

Payeng is not alone in his quest to plant more trees. Every year in the United States, people observe Arbor Day. On this day, Americans plant trees all around the country. People who can't plant trees can still do their part. They can plant flowers, vegetables, or bushes. Every little bit helps.

Payeng plants a tree in sand.

Photosynthesis

Trees use sunlight to change carbon dioxide and water into sugars and oxygen. The sugars help trees grow. People and animals breathe the oxygen. This process cleans the air for all.

Payeng walks in the Molai Forest.

Composting

When you throw stuff away, it goes from your house to a landfill. Food dumped into landfills begins to **rot**. As food rots, it releases methane gas. This gas is very bad for the planet. In fact, it traps much more heat on Earth than carbon dioxide does. So, lowering the amount of methane released is good for the planet and for the air we breathe.

This person puts food into his compost bin.

Instead of throwing away food, some cities are encouraging people to compost. Composting releases much less methane than landfills do. To compost, people put leftover food in a special box or container. Then, earthworms eat the food and turn it into soil. A lot of food comes from plants, which need soil to grow. When people compost food, they return it to the form it came from. Plus, they can use the soil to grow more food!

These earthworms create new soil.

How to Compost

Composting requires both *browns* and *greens*. Browns are things such as dead leaves, cut branches, and twigs. Greens are things such as fresh grass clippings, orange peels, and avocado pits.

Public Transportation

Vehicles let off a lot of **greenhouse gases**. So, people look for new ways to travel. They may use electric vehicles. More and more vehicles run on electricity. Or they may use **public transportation**. Some cities let people take bus routes for free. The goal is to get a lot of people to ride together on one bus instead of driving their own cars. That means the amount of greenhouse gases per person is lower. For each bus full of people, about half as much gas is released into the air as would be if those people drove their own cars!

bicycle traffic jam in the Netherlands

Other places encourage people to ride their bikes. For instance, people in the Netherlands love to bike. More than one-fourth of all travel there is done on bikes. Sometimes, there are so many bikes on the road that they cause **traffic jams**!

Finding Your Footprint

The total amount of greenhouse gases that a person is responsible for is called their *carbon footprint*. People can use websites to calculate their carbon footprint. Then, they can work to lower the impact of their footprint.

Reduce, Reuse, Recycle

When people make and deliver goods, gases are released into the atmosphere. For people who want to cut down on their carbon footprint, there are other options.

People can donate their clothes. Secondhand stores sell used clothes at a discount. When people buy used clothes, not as many new clothes need to be made. So, fewer greenhouse gases are released. Charities take used clothes too. They give them to people who need them.

Other people choose to **upcycle** their clothing. When people upcycle, they take things that would normally go in the trash and create new products. That may mean turning a shirt into a tote bag. Or people may turn towels into new toys for their pets. Upcycle That is a group that offers people ideas they can do at home. Their goal is to inspire people to think in new ways about waste.

Jeans have been upcycled into a purse.

Vintage Clothing

Instead of buying new clothes, some people choose to go to vintage stores. Vintage stores sell clothes from a previous time. Sometimes, these stores have styles of clothing that people can't find in other stores.

This woman shops at a secondhand store.

Plant-Based Diets

About 2.5 million years ago, humans began eating meat. It was an important part of their diet. Meat has protein, which humans need. So, for many years, meat was a large part of many people's diets.

With so many **carnivores**, there needed to be more cows. When cows burp, they let off methane gas. This gas makes the air dirty. So the more cows there are, the dirtier the air.

What's the Impact?

When farm animals are raised to make money, they are called *livestock*. They are one of the main causes of unclean air. Livestock let off almost one-fifth of the greenhouse gases in the world. Less livestock means cleaner air.

Some people choose to eat less or no meat as a way to help the environment. They think people should eat mostly foods that come from plants. This could be fruits, vegetables, beans, grains, and more.

Some companies are working to support this way of eating. They have invented plant-based foods that cook and taste like meat.

People can buy plant-based foods at grocery stores.

Fighting for Clean Air

Individuals can do their part to fight for clean air. But together, people can accomplish even more. In the United States, people have power. The government works for the people. People can write to their leaders. They can say they want clean air. Leaders represent the people. So, they listen to what people say.

Some people go a step further. They organize **protests** for clean air. They march and bring attention to the issue. There are lots of these events around the world. Everyone is welcome to join them.

These Americans demand clean air.

A crowd protests against pollution.

Contacting Lawmakers

Even though you can't vote yet, leaders still want to hear from you! You can call local, state, and national leaders. You can also write them letters or emails. These simple steps make a big difference.

All around the world, people are fighting for clean air. One major way they do this is by protecting the Amazon Rainforest.

The Amazon is known as the lungs of our planet. That is because it is home to almost 400 billion trees! More than one-fifth of the world's oxygen and water come from the Amazon. Unfortunately, in recent years, companies have begun cutting down lots of trees there. They want to build houses instead. And the Amazon is not the only forest this happens to. There are now half as many rainforests on Earth as there were 100 years ago.

Amazon Rainforest

Think and Talk

Why do you think this photo and the one on the right are shown here? What text supports your idea?

People are working to stop companies from cutting down trees. We need trees to make oxygen. We need trees to get rid of harmful gases too. The fewer trees our planet has, the dirtier the air is. People are fighting for laws that will protect the land. They speak out against those companies too.

cutting down trees in a rainforest

In 1963, the U.S. government passed the Clean Air Act. Under the law, the government works to keep air clean. At first, some people did not want to support this act. They thought that it would lead to new laws that would hurt businesses. But the Clean Air Act has made air cleaner. The United States now has one of the lowest pollution levels in the world.

Clean air affects everyone. Millions of people die each year due to health problems caused by dirty air. Each country has to do its part to fight pollution. Luckily, lots of world leaders agree. Many governments are investing in **clean energy**. They are offering more public transportation options. They are passing laws to cut down on pollution. Clean air is a global fight. It will take everyone to make it happen.

President Richard Nixon expands the power of the Clean Air Act in 1970.

Following the Law

In 1971, some lawyers formed a group called Earthjustice. This group makes sure that companies follow the Clean Air Act. They do not charge for their work! They rely on **donations**.

Solar and wind power are forms of clean energy.

Up to Us

Air does not become dirty on its own. Humans have the power to keep air clean or to make it dirty. It's important that people make good choices to keep our air clean. That way, people and animals around the world can be happy and healthy.

The United States has clean air. But it also adds a lot of greenhouse gases to the atmosphere. We can each do our part to make things better. People can stand up for clean air. They can work on lowering their carbon footprints. Americans can ask for laws to keep the air clean. The work for clean air is ongoing, and together we can make a difference.

Bike riding is celebrated in this yearly California event.

Students in Florida plant trees.

Think and Talk

Why is clean air important to you?

Glossary

carbon dioxide—a gas that is used by plants for energy

carnivores—meat eaters

clean energy—power that can be made without making air, water, or land dirty

donations—things such as money or food that people give to help other people or groups

greenhouse gases—gases that take in the sun's rays, trap heat, and add to the greenhouse effect

pollute—to make water, air, or land dirty and not safe to use

pollution—things that make water, land, or air dirty and not suitable or safe for use

protests—events at which people gather together to show they do not approve of or like things

public transportation—a group of vehicles, such as trains and buses, that are paid for or ran by the government

rot—to slowly break down naturally, or decay

traffic jams—times when long lines of vehicles on roads have stopped moving or are moving very slowly

upcycle—reusing objects in a way to make new products that are better than the originals

Index

Civics in Action

The American people do many things to care for the world. Their lawmakers can help too. They can pass new laws. These laws may help the air stay clean.

1. Think about why clean air is important.

2. Brainstorm ways lawmakers can help clean the air.

3. Find out who your local, state, or national lawmakers are.

4. Write a letter to one of your lawmakers about why clean air is important to you. Ask for their help.

5. Mail your letter!